THE MESSAGE OF
THE LORD'S PRAYER

THE MESSAGE OF
THE
LORD'S
PRAYER

BY

IGOR I. SIKORSKY

NEW YORK
CHARLES SCRIBNER'S SONS
1942

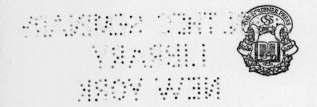

TO

★ *ELIZABETH SIKORSKY* ★

FROM TIME IMMEMORIAL, men have associated the sun and stars directly or figuratively with the idea of Divine Providence. The light and life-supporting power of the sun, as well as the quiet and mysterious beauty of the stars, appeared to reflect the ways and the will of God. Mankind, for thousands of years, attempted to read and interpret this heavenly message. A child or a primitive human soul would understand this message in his own way and would be impressed by the calm simplicity beyond which he could feel the solemn, mysterious greatness. A modern person who tried to learn and to think about it would feel the same, but would also realize with awe the immensity, splendor and dynamic power of the material heaven-universe of God.

The ideas outlined above are somewhat similar to the impression created in my consciousness by the Lord's Prayer with reference to the unseen realities of the spiritual universe. The few brief sentences consisting of some sixty-six words are simple and can be understood by a child. But when one starts to think and to analyze them carefully, there gradually comes the realization of the overwhelming immensity of the message. There comes the understanding that the Lord's Prayer not only states all that a human being should ask from his Creator, but indirectly throws light on several fundamental questions as to the meaning of our life, as well as our relation to God and the universe.

Besides being the fundamental Christian prayer for the church and home, the Lord's Prayer was particularly intended for the individual human being and to be pronounced in privacy and solitude.

In verses immediately preceding the Text, we can read (Matthew 6:6):

"But thou, when thou prayest, enter into thy
closet, and when thou hast shut thy door,
pray to thy Father which is in secret."

It would be difficult to emphasize more strongly that at least sometime a man must remain all alone and shut the door to outside influence when he boldly addresses this spiritual message directly to the Creator of the Universe.

Taking these instructions seriously, I started at a certain time in my life to study and analyze carefully the text of the Prayer in order to understand as much as I could the full meaning of the sentence which I was pronouncing. Often when walking alone through forests or climbing mountains, I thought about the great prayer until I began to realize that besides the direct meaning of the few outwardly simple sentences, the Prayer included indirectly a very extensive and profound message.

In the pages that follow, I have attempted to outline some personal ideas and conclusions on this subject.

December, 1941.   I. I. SIKORSKY.
Bridgeport, Connecticut.

★ CONTENTS ★

OUR FATHER *which art in heaven, Hallowed be thy name. Thy kingdom come. Thy will be done in earth, as it is in heaven. Give us this day our daily bread. And forgive us our debts, as we forgive our debtors. And lead us not into temptation, but deliver us from evil: For thine is the kingdom, and the power, and the glory, for ever.* AMEN.

(Matthew 6:9–13)

Modern electrical engineering knows how to send several different messages at the same time through a single wire. In a similar way the Founder of Christianity, besides excellent power and precision of speech, possessed a remarkable ability to place, when He wanted it, several meanings or messages into one sentence. As an illustration of this, we will take the discussion that preceded the telling of the Parable of the Vineyard (Luke 20:1–8).

The tragic conclusion of the earthly life of Christ was approaching, the rupture between Him and His adversaries was complete and they were using every opportunity to discredit and, if possible, to accuse Him. Once when He was preaching in the Temple the Chief Priests and the Elders approached Him and asked by what authority He did so.

The attack was clever and probably well planned. It happened on the grounds of the Temple where His adversaries were masters who assumed their right and duty to request some kind of proof from a person who preached in the temple and claimed to possess heavenly credentials for such action. The only convincing proof for the people who were assembled would be some demonstrative miracle. Moses could command the waters of the Red Sea to move away, he could make the earth open and swallow the men who dared to question his authority; Joshua could stop the sun from moving, and so forth. These and other similar stories were believed to be literally true by the people of that time, and it was then taken for granted that such miracles did really happen when a true messenger from Heaven needed confirmation of his authority.

The Chief Priests already had come to know that Christ never used His miraculous power for demonstration of personal importance. Therefore, they could expect that Christ either would give no answer at all or would be forced to enter into a theological argument with clever and unfair adversaries before an ignorant group of people, which would offer His enemies an opportunity to discredit and denounce Him. This plan, however, did not work. While Christ actually made no use of His supernatural powers, yet by a single sentence He proved His case and defeated His enemies to such an extent that they did not dare even to continue the discussion.

This reply, itself in the form of a question, was as follows:

"The Baptism of John, whence was it? from heaven, or of men?" (Matthew 21:25, Luke 20:4.)

This sentence included a complete reply and had three meanings conveying three different phases of the situation, which are, briefly:

First meaning—Christ mentioned the name of a Witness of His credentials whose integrity and authority no one dared to question. John the Baptist, who was already dead at that time, was considered by the people of Jerusalem to be a Prophet, yet it was known that he accepted Christ as being greater than himself.

Second meaning—Some of the people, while ready to listen to and accept Christ, may have been disturbed by the criticism and disbelief of the high priests. The same sentence would show them another case in which a man proved by his life and death that he was a prophet and still was not recognized by the priests.

Third meaning—The adversaries of Christ started the discussion in order to discredit Him. By the single sentence in the form of a question, Christ forced them to make a reply which reversed the whole situation. With reference to John the Baptist, it was their duty as Scribes and Priests either to recognize and accept a prophet or to denounce an impostor. If they were unable to distinguish between the two or if they had no courage to tell the truth, in either case they demonstrated that they did not deserve to be the religious leaders of the people.

Christ had demonstrated this outstanding ability of condensing a vast meaning or message into a short sentence on numerous occasions. Such expressions as "Render therefore unto Cæsar the things which are Cæsar's . . ." or, "He that is without sin among you, let him first cast a stone at her . . ." are well-known examples and are used even by non-believers. Thus, it could well be expected that in the prayer, which is one of the most important parts of ·the whole Gospel, an extensive, profound and important message and meaning would be embodied. There seems to be no doubt that this actually is the case.

With reference to the Lord's Prayer, I am a fundamentalist ready to accept every word and sentence in their full, direct, and complete meaning. All historical evidence leaves no doubt as to the Author of the prayer. Even if we imagine that by some accident the prayer had not been recorded in the authentic Gospel, but had reached mankind through some obscure and unreliable source, I am confident that there would be many sensitive and intelligent Christians who would recognize unmistakably the Author on the basis of the supreme spiritual value and power of the prayer. Therefore, the acceptance of the prayer as of human or superhuman origin would simply follow, the way we accept its Author. And we would be well justified in taking each word and each sentence in the most direct and precise, yet most extensive and profound meaning that we are able to discover.

The universal and outstanding importance of the prayer is well known. Hundreds of millions of people repeat it every day. To millions the Lord's Prayer may have been their major connection with religion. To many in exile or under persecution who may not have the Bible and may be unable to secure the needed guidance from a religious friend the prayer well remembered from childhood may become the only reliable link with the higher realities of life.

In view of these facts, we can easily understand why the Author placed in the prayer such vast and underlying meaning as not only covers all that a man can ask from his Creator but also indirectly discloses several major truths about God, man, and his place in the universe.

The Great Prayer was composed to be understood by a child or the simplest soul, to satisfy the spiritual needs, and also to guide the wisest and most learned until the end of time.

In the text of the prayer we find a careful selection of words and expressions so as to protect the true meaning against changes resulting from translations and from the effects of time. For instance, such words as *judge* or *despot* may have very dissimilar meanings at different times in history and when translated into various languages.

Yet in the Lord's Prayer we find all important words and sentences chosen in such a way as to preserve the meaning irrespective of the influence of time and translations into other languages. Such words as *father, kingdom, will, bread, temptation, earth,* and so forth, have a definite and identical meaning in all languages and centuries. It is true that some of the expressions and particularly the words *heaven* and *evil* represent very difficult subjects on which there exist a number of different opinions. But this controversy is not caused by the use of particular words or translations but by the deeply mysterious character of the subjects covered by each of these words.

The meaning of certain expressions of the Lord's Prayer is greatly widened by modern scientific information. I firmly believe, however, that this is a correct development and expansion of ideas which were always signified by the mysteriously powerful words of the prayer. The mentioning of the word *science* may need some clarification. In the past and sometimes even at present attempts have been made to discredit natural science in general because some of its discoveries appear to be in discord with Genesis or some other part of the Old Testament. While such tendencies formerly have retarded scientific progress, at present they are regrettable because they do harm to religion by associating it with ignorance. Without reopening the discussion of the so-called conflict between science and religion, or more correctly, theology, I would only mention that among the very first men to find and accept Christ were wealthy alien scientist-astronomers. To them belongs the enviable credit of having been among the first to recognize and worship Christ and also the first to render Him an important service, because their timely, valuable gifts undoubtedly helped Joseph to undertake the trip to Egypt that was necessary to save the life of the newly born Christ. While the direct meaning of the star of Bethlehem may never become known, the indirect meaning is clear and important. It states that science can guide men to God and to Christ.

It is true that most of the early Christians were not interested in the natural sciences. The reason for this we can easily understand. According to the conceptions of the vast majority of people of that time the earth was the most important body and the base of the universe, with the sun and the stars being only accessories to it. The early Christians believed that the earth would be destroyed very soon, probably during their own lifetime or shortly afterward. The catastrophe would be followed by the creation of a new earth, which, for them, meant practically a new universe. Our present ideas on this subject are quite different. The universe, in which the earth is only a minor speck, was found to be of immensely greater majesty, size and beauty. It has been in existence for probably hundreds of trillions of years and, according to reasonable thinking, its future is of a similar order of magnitude. While the destruction of the earth by fire was predicted in the New Testament, this future catastrophe may well be regarded as a local event of no importance outside the solar system. There is little doubt that the great, majestic and mysterious universe is here to stay for millions of millions of years as a visible monument to the power and wisdom of its Creator. Not without purpose is it opened to our observation and study by the miraculous faculty of eyesight combined with the relatively rare characteristics of the earthly atmosphere that permit observing and studying heavenly bodies. And while any thinking human being must be interested in it simply because of its majesty and beauty, a religious person must, besides that, be interested because of reverence and love for its Creator.

An elderly and well-respected teacher in the naval academy where I was studying once asked me whether I had read the books written by my father, and he added with great emphasis that a son *must* be interested in the creative work of his father. This wise suggestion is, I believe, directly applicable to the case of a religious person who considers the Creator of the Universe to be his Heavenly Father. What would we say of a son of Raphael or Shakespeare, if he existed, if he were not interested in looking at or in reading the work of his father? Or what would we say of a commentator, speaking to us about Thomas Edison, who would use written biographical data, but would disregard completely the creative work of Edison as being unimportant or at least not deserving any consideration? The reason for mentioning these ideas while discussing a religious subject will be seen later.

Analyzing the structure of the Lord's Prayer, we see at first the finished symmetric composition that facilitates holding it in the memory. A child will learn and remember verses much more easily than prose, even though he may not yet know the difference. Verse form would be out of place for the prayer because of the solemn seriousness of the subject and because it was obviously intended to be translated into hundreds of different languages; but the beautiful symmetry of a finished mathematical formula was well suited.

In the following arrangement several interesting facts about its structure can be recognized readily:

Our Father
which art in heaven,

The address

1. Hallowed be thy name.
2. Thy kingdom come.
3. Thy will be done in earth,
    as it is in heaven.

The first Prayer deals mainly with final eternal destinies of mankind in relation to God and universe.

1. Give us this day our daily bread.
2. And forgive us our debts,
    as we forgive our debtors.
3. And lead us not into temptation,
    but deliver us from evil:

The second Prayer deals mainly with material and spiritual needs of the present time.

For thine is the kingdom,
and the power, and the glory,
for ever. AMEN.

The conclusion.

Whatever meaning we would attribute to numbers, it is known that three and seven are prominently displayed in all religions. The Lord's Prayer is composed substantially on these two numbers. Besides the words of address, it consists of seven definite propositions, which in turn represent two separate prayers of three sentences each, and a conclusion.

The three sentences of the second prayer refer to the present time and to our earthly level of life while the rest of the prayer deals mainly with a higher order of existence and events. The inspired writers of olden times would call this higher order eternity. This is in thorough agreement with modern ideas, only now we would understand eternity not as an endless repetition of days and centuries but as a life in a higher order of existence, above the limitations of time.

In analyzing the Lord's Prayer, we will follow this division into two parts and will study separately each sentence, attempting to understand besides its direct meaning, also what may be considered as the message that is disclosed indirectly or is reflected in the profoundly significant words of this greatest of prayers.

I

T IS DIFFICULT to realize to the full extent the immense importance of the first two words of the prayer. Seldom can a whole volume communicate such a profoundly significant message as is included in these two words.

The expression "Our Father" is familiar to us; the prayer itself is often referred to by these two words, and we are somewhat used to pronouncing them mechanically without truly realizing their deep meaning. A large part of the medieval and even some of the contemporary religious conceptions are in discord with the plain meaning of these words. To harmonize with these familiar conceptions, the addressing words should have been "Our eternal dictator and stern judge," but, thank God, this is not the case.

The words, "Our Father," determine and explain the relationship that exists between God and man by comparing it with a very familiar kind of human relationship. An overwhelming feeling of optimistic confidence and brightest hope is created in the heart of every one who accepts these words seriously in their full meaning.

As a rule, a good human father is a most benevolent person to his child. In general, he provides all that is required for the life and development of his offspring, usually expecting to receive little or nothing in return. A father may, when necessary, inflict temporary punishment in order to improve the character and personality of his child, but he will never cause suffering unless he believes that it will bring lasting benefit. The greatest permanent punishment which a good human father may consider, no matter what the guilt, would be to disown his sinful offspring and order him to go away and never to return.

Believing and realizing that even the best and noblest earthly father must be in every respect incomparably below the Heavenly One, a human being may get immense spiritual comfort from the authorization to address the Lord of the Universe by the words, "Our Father."

It is necessary to recognize the fact, however, that not all human beings can be considered the children of God. In one of the severest statements of the Gospel, Christ said to a group of adversaries, "Ye are of your father the devil, and the lusts of your father ye will do. He was a murderer from the beginning, and . . . a liar" (John 8:44). This was the reply to a confident claim, "We have one Father, even God" (John 8:41).

A sentence so precise and stern as this cannot be disregarded. It plainly indicates that among human beings some are the children of God, while others are not. There is no doubt, however, that besides the two extreme and definite groups, there is a third one which probably describes the position of the majority of mankind. This seems to be indicated by the well-known parable of the wandering son. The young man in the story used his freedom by going away with his share of wealth and "wasted his substance with riotous living" (Luke 15:13). The logical meaning of the story is, however, that while the young man was living in such a manner he did not become the son of the devil or even of the drunkards or gamblers in whose company he was spending his time and wealth. He remained always the son of his father, and only by going away did he separate himself from receiving the guidance and help of his father. He finally got into distress and danger, realized his faults, came back and was accepted by his father who expressed great joy and said to the other son, "For this thy brother was dead, and is alive again; and was lost, and is found" (Luke 16:32).

No attempt will be made to discuss this vast subject in general, but in connection with the ideas inspired by the Lord's Prayer the fundamental question is this: Can it happen that a human being will stretch his hands to God and pronounce, "Our Father," with faith and hope, and yet the prayer will get nowhere because the particular person may happen to be one who is not entitled to address God as "Our Father"? And is there an authority who can decide, or a rule that would indicate whether a given person can address God as "Our Father"?

The sincere beliefs of the writer on this subject are as follows:

The guidance of the church and of individual preachers is extremely valuable and helpful in order to assist a man in his spiritual ascent, but no authority or institution on earth can grant or deny a human being the right and opportunity to address God as "Our Father."

The whole question is one of a strictly inner spiritual nature between God and the individual man.

Furthermore, several statements of Christ and, still more, His acts, justify the brightest hopes in this connection. The young man in the parable or the woman taken in sin, and even the thief on the cross who probably had burglaries and murders on his conscience, were all forgiven without even a verbal censure. All of these were considered as lost children of God and not as offspring of the devil.

But if this is the case, who then are the unfortunate ones whom Christ addressed with the terrible words, "Ye are of your father the devil" . . .? Without attempting to justify the conclusion by philosophical or scriptural reference, the writer will briefly outline his personal beliefs on this subject.

Among the various trespasses and faults that separate man from God, it is possible to recognize two general groups, the ones that point to the weaknesses of man and others that point to proud, self-contented power of evil. The latter group seems to be the more serious and dangerous. It can be recognized mainly by a deliberate hatred of Christ and an insult to His divine power. The warning of Matthew 12:31: "All manner of sin and blasphemy shall be forgiven unto men: but the blasphemy against the Holy Ghost shall not be forgiven unto men," was addressed to a group of Pharisees who said that Christ cast out devils by an evil power. Similarly, the sentence, "Ye are of your father the devil," mentioned earlier, was addressed to men who said to Christ: "Say we not well that thou . . . hast a devil?" (John 8:48). The greatest danger, therefore, is connected with the deliberate hatred, insults and mockery of the divine power and personality of Christ. It is obvious that a person who has such feelings would not pray the Lord's Prayer anyway.

This being the case, the writer faithfully believes that no permission can be given or denied by any earthly authority and that none is needed for the use of the greatest prayer. Any human being who has confidence, faith and love for Christ can "enter into a closet, shut the door and pray to the Father which is in secret" with a happy and bold hope that his spiritual message will reach its highest destination.

THE SOLEMN and profound meaning of this sentence is felt inwardly rather than discussed in words. I believe that it is pronounced in connection with the present life and still more with the final destinies and the future higher order of existence. It also seems to have another meaning and purpose. By being permitted to call the Creator of the Universe, "Father," man may start to think about himself more than he is entitled to. This second sentence which man pronounces reverently, lovingly, and by his own will, as if taking an oath for this life and for eternity, returns him where he belongs. That place is extremely modest compared with the position of the One to whom he pledges eternal reverence.

It is my firm belief, based on logic and intuition, that men of this earth are by no means the only or the highest conscious living beings that pronounce a sentence of such nature. While a system of planets near a star must be regarded as a rare exception, yet in view of the immense multitude of stars in the universe, there is hardly any doubt that at least some must have a family of planets and it is probable that there may be other inhabited worlds besides our earth. As long as the subject of religion is understood not as a product of human imagination but as a supreme reality revealed by the Divine Power, it would be only natural to expect that living beings spiritually enlightened by the same Divine Providence and intellectually developed under the same fundamental laws of the Universe would express in a similar way their reverence to their Creator.

Religious ideas of all times indicate that besides our material kind of life there are also higher grades of spiritual beings that are believed to be immortal, to be free from all limitations and needs connected with our physical existence, to be independent of gravitation, capable of appearing wherever they want, or rushing through space faster than lightning. These higher beings, whose reality can only be an object of faith, because it can be neither proved nor disproved, do not pray about the kingdom to come because they already live in the Kingdom of God. But seeing and realizing the power and glory of the Divine heaven-universe as we cannot even dream or imagine, they most certainly also express their reverent devotion in a way which, if reduced to the meager possibilities of human language, would probably best be expressed by the same words, "Hallowed be Thy Name."

In pronouncing the Lord's Prayer, we reunite ourselves with all the hundreds of millions of Christians of the earth and even with all of mankind because all men are in need of the objectives that are asked in the Lord's Prayer even though many do not realize it. But the words, "Hallowed be Thy Name," figuratively remove the limitations of our little planet. In pronouncing them, we feel ourselves to be members of some immense family of conscious beings of various grades that inhabit the Universe and are reunited by the act of expressing reverent praise to their common Creator and Father.

THE TWO remaining sentences of the first prayer are mentioned together because they are interrelated, referring to the same idea and supporting each other. Actually, one of the simplest yet most correct ways of explaining what a kingdom is would be to say that it is a place or a large body of people among whom the will of a King is being done.

These sentences may be understood as our prayer that the will of God, as explained by Christ, would be gradually adopted by men, bringing peace and harmony on the earth. Such explanation is true, but I believe it discloses only a secondary meaning, while the main and most important meaning is different and points to a definite event that would close for the individual, and eventually for the whole of mankind, the temporary, earthly era of compromise and suffering and would open a fundamentally different one that is called the Kingdom of Heaven.

Analyzing the true and full meaning of "Thy kingdom come," we find two important messages. In order to "come," it is necessary that the object be,

(*a*) Not yet in the place under discussion;

(*b*) In existence in some other place from which it is expected to come.

These two conclusions are obligatory, logical consequences if the word *come* is used correctly, which no doubt is the case. If we were to assume that the kingdom in question is not yet in existence somewhere, then the correct phrase would be "Thy kingdom" be created or established, but not "come." If, on the other hand, a Kingdom of God of the kind that is referred to in the prayer were conceived as already existing on the earth, then it would be logical to ask for its continuance or victorious expansion, and the word *come* would not be thoroughly accurate. Therefore, the meaning attributed to the word *come* appears to be correct.

This idea is further confirmed and clarified by the next sentence, "Thy will be done in earth as it is in heaven." The first six words of this sentence taken alone could be understood as pointing to the best of mankind that will gradually learn to live and act on this earth in conformity with the will of God. But the remaining part of the sentence permits a wider and more encouraging interpretation. While good men living in accord with the will of God always did exist on the earth, yet they were and always will be in the minority. In general, the prevailing quality of life on earth was and will be a mixture of good and evil.

I believe that this conclusion is well in line with the message of the New Testament. Every single writer quoting Christ, as well as expressing his own beliefs, foresees wars, persecution, hatred, and chaos. I believe, therefore, that the sentence "as it is in heaven" was placed in the prayer in order to warn us from accepting these two fundamental verses as referring to anything that can be achieved in the heart of one or many people, while the present stage of the historical process is under way. Facing the truth as it is and recognizing basic facts about human nature and history, we must come to the somewhat gloomy conclusion that the highest achievements to be expected in the future under the most optimistic assumptions will always be a sort of temporary truce, a compromise between good and evil, right and wrong.

The last five words, "as it is in heaven," are believed to determine the meaning of the sentences. The Kingdom of God may and does exist in the hearts of some pure human beings, but the Lord's Prayer permits and encourages us to pray not only for this but also for an infinitely higher and happier objective.

When Christ was dying, His mother, His beloved disciple and a few distressed followers were standing near the Cross. They most certainly had faith in their loyal courageous hearts, but outwardly they were helpless, and the whole immense tragedy was also the symbol of the Kingdom of God as it is on the earth. The dark forces that incited a misguided mob to shout for the death of Christ are today just as evil, active and aggressive as they were two thousand years ago. Under the unreliable and powerless outer polish of civilization, there is the same vicious beast with lust for power and readiness to spill streams of innocent tears and blood in order to conquer or to retain domination over gold and over men.

There are also today human beings who are peacemakers, merciful and idealistic. And these, the best among mankind, are frequently stretching their hands to heaven and screaming in physical or mental agony, "O, God, why hast thou forsaken us?" Their cries and prayers are addressed to the Heavenly Power, which, according to all tangible earthly evidence, remains indifferent to their suffering, just as it appeared indifferent to the few distressed men and women with the Kingdom of God in their broken hearts who watched the life of Christ slowly fade from a tormented body and who listened to the laughter and mockery of triumphant wickedness. Such is the Kingdom of God as it is on the earth, and the terrible moral downfall of mankind which we are witnessing forces the conclusion that the so-called progress of humanity within the present level of life holds no hopes for any reliable and worthy achievements even in the future.

More than that, at critical periods the spark of the Kingdom of God in the heart is itself liable to become a source of suffering. Christ ordered His followers to carry their crosses. The meaning of this is more than carrying with patience the burden of life. A cross is not only a heavy load, but it is an instrument by which torture and death are to be inflicted on the one who carries it. Faithful bearing of a cross brings the realization that the little flame of divine light in the heart of an individual human being is unable to conquer the powerful, aggressive darkness roundabout. It only sharpens the understanding that truth and goodness are condemned in this world to mockery and persecution. It forces the realization that the voice of true idealism is barely noticeable in this world, while triumphant wickedness is powerfully entrenched in places of influence; evil boldly stares from the headlines of newspapers, it thunders its propaganda of lies and hatred from all radio loudspeakers of the old world and the new. And the achievements of science and progress which raised immensely the material standards of living and furnished mankind with wonderful mechanical toys—electricity, the airplane, radio and so forth, have proved in the final analysis to be hopelessly powerless to lift mankind spiritually or morally.

Of the thousands of cases that illustrate this conclusion, let us take just one. Deliberate murder of a defenseless child who stretched its little arms and begged for mercy appeared to be revolting to men who had at least some human feeling left in their heart. Nineteen centuries ago Herod ordered the slaughter of a number of small children because he thought, and not without reason from his standpoint, that this was necessary in order to protect his political power. This act was generally considered as one of the greatest crimes in human history. Poets and artists, preachers and philosophers, condemned it with all the vigor and power at their command.

Yet in this twentieth century of enlightenment and civilization, our modern Herods, for the same objective of fighting for new or protecting the existing political domination, proved ready and willing to blast the lives of thousands upon thousands of innocent, defenseless children with bombs or to extinguish these lives by a torturing hunger blockade. They cover their acts by appropriate explanations; they are all being done invariably for the final blessing of humanity, the triumph of righteousness and whatnot. Because, after all, are not the means justified by the ends?

In the light of moral principles and certainly from the Christian standpoint, means are frequently more important than ends. Therefore, when such crimes against mankind take place, the divine flame, while remaining a source of comfort, becomes also a source of sorrow, because it sharpens the realization and understanding of the deep and hopeless inner tragedy of mankind. On the pages of the Gospel, we find a sentence of the devil who said that all the power and glory of the earthly kingdoms are delivered unto him and that he is giving them to whomsoever he wishes (Luke 4:6). In the face of the present moral bankruptcy of civilized humanity, this bold claim assumes a sinister reality.

Traditional religion explains such moral degradation by referring to original sin, freedom of will and the knowledge of good and evil, but a human soul that is in bewilderment and despair may not be satisfied with such explanation. Though we assume that all grown-ups are really sinners and deserve all the misery they suffer, there are still the thousands of innocent children whose anguish is unexplained. If this is the tuition fee for the understanding of good and evil, then the expenses may seem too high for the course, particularly because mankind, after having studied for thousands of years and having paid this disastrously high price, appears yet to have progressed very little beyond the ideals of Cain. The watchword of a stern British admiral was: "Hit first, hit hard, keep on hitting."[1] Such rules may be inevitable in battle, but at the present time the ideas embodied in them become more and more the accepted normal principle of relation between peoples

[1] See *Atlantic Monthly,* June, 1941, page 680.

who are not at war. If Cain were to come back again he would probably exclaim, "O, my children, I could not have said it better."

In what are considered normal peaceful times, when civilized politeness and traditional hypocrisies prevent us from seeing the evil beast, we become ready to deny its reality and to think that all inhumanity is a question of the remote past. It is easy then to have faith in the triumph of progress and idealism. But at a time of crisis, the divine flame in the heart may become a light that may guide towards a cross and a Calvary which may be quite real even if they are only mental. Those who are spiritually great and personally strong can endure such a cross, although it may call for all their faith and courage. Not only men, but even Christ, with His superhuman power, was overburdened in the Garden of Gethsemane and later on the Cross when He exclaimed, "O, My God, why hast thou forsaken me?" Christ and the greatest among His followers remained loyal and faithful to God, Who appeared outwardly to have "forsaken them," to have left them defenseless in the hands of triumphant wickedness. But this inner act of supreme spiritual heroism may be beyond the power of a weaker human being in spite of his faith and idealism. The apparent indifference of the divine power with respect to the triumphant wickedness may cause heart-break and rebellion even against heaven itself. This is probably the extreme in human revolt and despair.

It is not the revolt of the self-reliant, radical dreamers whose success usually means the replacement of a weak government by a wicked one and who immediately proceed to break every one and all of their idealistic pledges as soon as they get power. Neither is it the shallow revolt of an atheist who may be sincere in denying the existence of God because his crippled or undeveloped spiritual being may be blind to the higher realities of the universe. There is no God for him as there is no God for a stone or for a mule.

It is the supreme spiritual revolt of a human being with faith and ideals whose confidence in the ways of God was shaken by the unbearable sight of triumphant evil.

This very abyss of human doubt and despair was explored by the genius of Dostoyevsky in his novel, *The Brothers Karamazov.*[2] In one of the discussions, the main hero, Ivan, expressed his feelings in the following way:

"I renounce the higher harmony altogether. . . . It is not worth the tears of that one tortured child who beat itself on the breast with its little fist and prayed . . . with its unexpiated tears to dear kind God. . . . And if the sufferings of children go to swell the sum of suffering which was necessary to pay for truth, then I protest that the truth is not worth such a price. . . . It's not God that I don't accept, only I most respectfully return Him the ticket."

The way in which these ideas were presented may be considered as overstressing the dark side of existence. Nevertheless, the reality and permanence of this aspect of earthly life cannot be denied. When the strain becomes too great, a human soul may become discouraged and bewildered. It will doubt, not only the higher quali-

[2]Random House, Modern Library edition, page 254.

ties of human beings and the destiny of mankind, but even the moral value and meaning of the whole creative process with respect to life on earth.

A doubt that results from an earnest, sincere, and idealistic search for truth is a legitimate and reasonable human reaction. When Saint Thomas expressed doubt in the face of the unanimous testimony of ten other disciples, Christ did not condemn him, but gave him the very kind of direct proof that he wanted. And in the face of this immense and tragic question the human soul has the right to seek an explanation.

Religious and philosophical thought from time immemorial has tried to understand the causes of the suffering of the innocent and of the triumph of the wicked. Many times the question was pronounced insoluble. In other cases solutions were proposed, none of which, however, was thoroughly convincing.

The traditional fundamentalist explanation argued that all the misery of living creatures was started by the original sin of Adam and Eve. Prior to it, both men and animals were living in a paradise where suffering, violence and death were unknown. It was the sin of man that brought the curse of suffering and death on himself and upon the whole animal kingdom. The story of the fall of man in the Bible undoubtedly presents a great mystery, whose interpretation is in need of revision. We know at present that whatever man did individually or collectively he is not responsible for the fact that violence and death are the general rule in the natural kingdom. They were firmly established on the earth for hundreds of millions of years before man made his appearance. Therefore, contrary to the old traditional ideas, man is not the cause of physical evil in nature, but rather is one of the victims of it.

This fact supports a pessimistic point of view. It would seem that the efforts of the few idealists who appear among mankind from time to time hardly can be expected to reverse the fundamental principles which nature has been steadily hammering into all living creatures on the earth for a hundred million years. However, the inner meaning and spirit of the message of Christ, together with at least a small, but truly divine flame in the heart, would inspire and justify a completely different understanding.

The despair and revolt which were mentioned earlier, actually never result from a truly divine flame and faith. Pessimism and bitterness may result from the earthly substitute of the Kingdom of God in the heart, from worldly idealism and sentimentalism which have an outward similarity to the divine spark, but do not possess even a minor fraction of its power. The true divine spark in the heart, besides increasing immensely the ability of a man to understand the meaning and mysteries of life, is always a source of the greatest comfort and courage. It does so in spite of any visible triumph of evil because it stresses the infinite importance and reality of the eternal. This flame makes one understand that God is not far away, not indifferent, but close, watching and seeing all; more than that, it reveals Him as helping and supporting in case of a crisis, although, as a general rule, not in a visible, material way.

But there has been given one direct reply and explanation whose thunderous power is well in line with

the scale of the question about the suffering of the innocent and the triumph of evil. It is the reply given by Christ
in His message and in His acts. Calvary and the tragic
events that immediately preceded it must be considered
as the greatest possible mental and physical agony which
any human being could be called to suffer in this life.
Yet Christ voluntarily accepted them. Whatever verbal
argument can be presented to deny or explain the meaning of the suffering of the innocent, Christ confirmed the
existence of such meaning by wilfully accepting the greatest possible suffering. He would have been able to avoid
the cross not only by His miraculous power but even by
natural means. But instead of that He went to Jerusalem
on the last visit against the advices of His followers, knowing what would happen; and He actually instigated the
tragedy by telling Judas, "That thou doest, do quickly"
(John 13:27). The chain of events that were started by
Calvary brought the supreme glory of resurrection which
in turn caused the greatest spiritual and even intellectual
rebirth that ever happened on earth. Yet even these immense visible results must be considered as incidental, because the true objectives of the ministry of Christ are
mostly in the higher, eternal plan of life and not in the
present temporary one.

Profoundly comforting ideas about the meaning and outcome of the sorrowful process of earthly life
are indirectly suggested in the Lord's Prayer. If we were
to assume that the text in question would read, "Thy kingdom come, thy will be done in the earth," that would
form a complete and finished logical sentence, but the
meaning would be entirely different. Then it would be

necessary to study on the basis of the scripture or of other reasonable evidence what can be the meaning of this future Kingdom of God on the earth, the coming of which was to be the object of our prayer.

But the text points definitely in another direction. It makes no mention of any earthly evils or injustices, it proposes or promises no divine or human cure for them; it disregards them completely as being of no permanent importance, as being destined to self-destruction and, therefore, as having no reality from the standpoint of the eternal. The Lord's Prayer instructs us to desire and pray for the Kingdom of God *as it is in heaven*. The last five words are a definition which determines the object of our prayer.

Attributing great importance to this sentence, I will try to analyze its meaning. Logically the phrase is similar, for instance, to the following: The course of studies must be arranged, "as it is in Yale University." This would indicate that a person interested in that question would have to find out how things were done in Yale University.

Leaving discussion of scriptural evidence to more competent students, I will turn to another source of information. While usually omitted from religious discussions, the realities which will be mentioned represent, to my mind, not only legitimate but obligatory evidence. A man of the past or a modern child if asked where heaven is would usually put the finger up, which I believe is pointing in the right direction. The sacred literature, as well as modern astronomy call the sun, moon and stars heavenly bodies. It is true that in general the traditional Christian doctrine would see no relation between the heaven of an astronomer and the heaven of the religious person. In this respect the religious doctrine would follow the conclusions of the early Christians who were greatly influenced by their belief that the earth was the foundation of the universe with the sun and stars being created as accessories to it.

This universe of theirs was a small structure created, as they thought during six days some four thousand years earlier. It went wrong almost from the beginning and was then expected soon to be torn down, destroyed by fire and replaced by a completely new structure. To a modern enlightened person the general outlook is different. The universe created or recharged with energy probably a few hundred trillion years ago in all probability will remain in existence for a duration of time of similar order. Its greatness and splendor are generally beyond our faculties of comprehension. With the little we know we have already discovered numerous instances of beauty and engineering precision simply unthinkable when compared with our own highest achievements.

The sun and stars which are the light and power generating stations of the universe are designed to operate with efficiency undreamt of by an engineer on the earthly planet. If we would know how to utilize the energy of combustibles in the way in which it is done in the sun, we could send a large steamer several times across the ocean on one pound of fuel.

I mention these ideas because I believe that the word *universe* should be understood in its higher meaning as very close, not to say identical, to the word *heaven*. I must recognize that this may involve rearranging several traditional ideas on that subject. I must also say that it must not be taken in a more direct sense than what is reasonable. Through our telescopes we do not see the heaven of a religious person, but we see the immense material framework of some mysterious structure, the meaning and purpose of which is beyond our understanding, but which undeniably has been created by God and functions in accord with His Will. And while what we see are obviously only the events of material character, yet in some cases an inner conviction leads me to believe these to be also shadows of events of higher order that happen in accord with a certain Will, as it is in Heaven. While I emphatically believe this to be true, yet my own attempt to interpret this message is far from complete or satisfactory and it is here offered with the hope that others will improve upon it.

The modern scientist can hardly predict rain for the next day with one hour's precision. Usually morning or afternoon is the best that can be done. With reference to heavenly events, scientists will predict the time and place of visibility of an eclipse with a precision of minutes and miles thousands of years ahead. This suggests wonderful *order* just as the efficiency of the sun and stars suggest wisdom and intelligence in their design.

The Founder of Christianity placed a great emphasis on freedom. How could this be combined with the wonderful order assumed in our analogy with visible heavenly mechanisms? On the earth, order and efficiency are almost inevitably associated with discipline and restriction of liberty. Turning again for some analogy into material machines, earthly and heavenly, we find an indication which I believe has a deep significance. In earthly mechanics, we use bolts, tie rods, cables, etc., to force the mechanism to stay together. A broken bolt or cable in an airplane may mean disaster. When a ship tows another it is done with a cable fixed to hooks or rings while all the other parts of the ship which do not "participate" are "indifferent." A broken cable or ring would send the ships apart. The heavenly mechanisms are operated on a radically different basic principle. The earth is moving around the sun and is guided on its orbit by an enormous gravitational force of about three and one-half million trillion tons. Contrary to the case of the two ships and the rope, in the heavenly bodies it is every particle which individually and independently attracts every one and all others in the same as well as in other heavenly bodies. Every grain of sand and every single drop of water "feels" and is attracted by all and every single particle of the sun. Every drop of blood in our body is attracted by every fiery drop of the hot solar material. The same is true with the heat and light which are sent out not by the sun as a whole, but rather are contributed by every particle of it so as to make our physical life possible. It is not a work under enforced discipline. It is rather a team work, a free and voluntary co-operation of countless trillions of trillions of particles, each of them free, yet all together maintaining the miraculous precision of the operation of the heavenly mechanisms that permit prediction of an astronomic event within a few seconds thousands of years ahead.

In all the machines created by man we find more or less friction that develops heat and lowers the efficiency of the mechanism. In a figurative way, the same is true to a much greater extent with reference to our human activities. When co-ordination of efforts and collaboration is needed between different groups or classes of men within a country or between various nations in this world, it is a general rule that "frictions" develop which invariably produce "heat" and reduce considerably the efficiency and results of activities. Referring to the events in the astronomical heaven, we find that bodies of an enormous mass are travelling with considerable velocity and as a general rule with practically complete absence of any friction.

The operation of the heavenly machines suggest some vague ideas about what may be happening in the order next above the visible material universe, with attraction or gravitation replaced by good will and love in its higher meaning. We can imagine multitudes of intelligent and powerful living beings of an order higher than our own dwelling and acting in this heaven-universe completely free yet in absolute harmony, reunited among themselves and united each and all of them with the Lord of the Universe by an overwhelming feeling of good will. It is into this company that Christ invited us and opened the door by His words, acts and sacrifice. The words, "Thy kingdom come, thy will be done in earth as it is in heaven," must be understood as a prayer that the life in full harmony with the will of God, which the Lord's Prayer tells us to believe already exists in the universe, would also descend and engulf our earth. The best part of mankind would then be lifted to the higher order of existence.

Our analogy with the material astronomical heaven suggests one more thought, this time of a tragic and sinister character. We realize that material particles all hold together in this universe by mutual gravitational force, and that it is this very attraction that causes and controls the wonderful reliability and precision of the operation of heavenly mechanisms. But what would happen to a particle that would not have preserved or would have lost the power of attraction—if such a particle should exist? This we can very well imagine. Driven by pressure of light, such a particle would be chased away from the sun, out of the solar system, away from our island universe, away from all the nebulæ because their number is limited and the size of the whole material universe is also believed to be limited. Away from all light and life into cold, dead darkness. A modern astronomer would, with excellent scientific precision, say that it would be driven into "outer darkness." Modern scientists believe that space is somewhat interdependent with matter and gravitation. This can be understood as meaning that where there is no matter there also would be no gravitation and no space, and the particle deprived of attraction and driven out would have to be considered, not only practically but even scientifically, as annihilated.

This probably presents some analogy with the tragic destiny of the unfortunate ones who have not developed in themselves under the divine guidance, the qualities that are required and necessary for permanent existence in the Kingdom of God. As far as I remember, Tolstoi said

that "Sin is not what a man did, but what he became."
While Dostoyevsky called the Devil the wise and dreadful
spirit of self-destruction and non-existence.[3]

The idea of Hell as a place which God designed and in which He provided equipment and personnel
necessary for a deliberate, perpetual torture of a multitude
of His unfortunate creatures is, to my mind, unacceptable.
But it appears quite certain that to the happy, everlasting
future life in heaven there is a tragic, desperate alternative.
It is the outer darkness, gradual self-destruction into non-
existence—final death.

The term self-destruction must not in this case
be understood as being similar to suicide. The feeling and
recognition of melting away into darkness and the final
death of the soul and individual personality after having
realized most probably the glory of everlasting life will
be one of supreme despair incomparably greater than anything that can be experienced by a prisoner condemned to
execution in this life. The latter realizes that his loss is
limited to a maximum of a few decades of earthly existence
and that there still may be hope for the future after the
death of the body, while for the former there would be the
realization of the immensity of the loss and the definite
absence of any hope.

The subject of eternal punishment is a serious,
controversial question. The very term may be understood
equally well in two different ways, namely, as final, absolute death, or as a resurrection into an everlasting life of
agony. Separate texts of the Scripture can be found
to support either of the two propositions and there are

[3]*The Brothers Karamazov*, Modern Library, Random House, page 261.

sincere Christians who still insist on the reality of endless torture in hell. However, not long ago, sincere and apparently competent students of the Scripture in a similar way have quoted confidently Bible texts to defend absurd scientific doctrines, to justify burnings at the stake, to protest against vaccination, to condemn severely attempts to reduce suffering at childbirth, and so forth. These, and a number of other facts of similar nature, place a question mark on the very method of using selected texts of the Scripture in a way in which a lawyer handles accepted evidence in court.

The real inner religious meaning must be found not in a legal or even logical investigation of separate expressions, but rather in the spirit of the whole Gospel truth as given and as personified by Christ. A final universe inhabited by truth, love and eternal happiness, in which all evil, all darkness, all suffering, were permanently eliminated would be in complete harmony with this spirit. A universe in which agony would be deliberately inflicted and endlessly perpetuated would be in contradiction to it.

In explaining and illustrating his ideas about the Kingdom of Heaven, the writer made use of known facts about the structure of the material universe. This method is believed to be reasonable. The achievements and ideas of men and the whole history of mankind reflect, besides the divine design, the turbulent and chaotic will of men, as well as some dark, vicious influence. Contrary to that, the sun, stars and all fundamental rules that control the operation of the material universe must be considered by a religious person to reflect directly the design

and the will of God and of no one else. And while no conclusions should be reached except with most respectful
care, yet it is only logical to expect that the ideas of the
Designer would be reflected in His creative work, just as
among human beings the ideas of an artist or architect may
usually be recognized in his creation.

Certain fundamental characteristics of the
material universe may suggest by analogy the solution to
the question that has been mentioned earlier about the
future destinies of mankind after the end of the historical
process. The question could be formulated as follows:
Should it be accepted that the justice of God would necessitate that, in line with eternal blessing and happiness to
part of humanity, there must also exist an endless agony
of comparable intensity for the rest of mankind? Or should
it be accepted that the infinite wisdom, goodness and love
of God will be reflected in the fact that the total volume
and intensity of happiness of His creatures would be infinitely greater than the total amount of sorrow and agony
connected with the creative process, and in particular with
the consequences of the free will of men, because the latter
must be considered as much a part of the divine plan as
electricity or gravitation?

Mathematics knows no difference between the
positive and negative. Any figure and even infinity can be
assumed with the sign of plus or minus. In his imagination,
man would feel himself in the middle with, say, positive
infinity of any mathematical nature stretching itself infinitely far away in one direction, while negative infinity
would also appear infinitely far away in the opposite
direction.

With reference to the material universe, the word "infinite" seems to be theoretically out of place. As far as we know, space, amount of matter and energy, light, and so forth, are all finite. However, most of the items reach such scales and dimensions that from the practical earthly standpoint they can be considered infinite.

Now in analyzing the major fundamental characteristics of the material universe we can draw interesting conclusions. Taking the case of light versus darkness, it would be reasonable to associate light with life, goodness, happiness, and darkness with evil, agony and death. It is obvious that the possible scale and intensity of each of them are absolutely different. Man can artificially create light of certain power. The sun is a countless number of times more powerful than any light that ever could be created by man. And there are stars that are tens of thousands of times more luminous than the Sun. To all practical value, there is light in the universe which is infinitely greater than any that is within the scale of man. The expression "immensely or infinitely powerful light" has a sound practical meaning.

With reference to darkness, it is all different. The expression "immense or infinite darkness" would have no meaning. Just complete darkness is all that there would be. If a man descended in a mine or tunnel only a few hundred feet below the ground he would find there nearly as complete darkness as there may be in the very "outer darkness." Therefore, contrary to the case of mathematics, man is not at all in the middle, he is at the very bottom. He can see and feel the conditions that from every practical standpoint resemble darkness as complete as it exists. It is well within his reach. But light may be immensely and incomparably greater than anything that he could reproduce or observe or even endure.

The case is similar with respect to heat. The highest temperature created by man is between three and four thousand degrees centigrade, which is the heat of some electric furnaces. Now the temperature inside the Sun is believed to be around forty million degrees. It is still higher in some other stars. These temperatures are immensely higher than any that can be reproduced by man. But with reference to cold, the case is again completely different. While the expression "million" or forty million degrees above the freezing point has a perfect reality, yet the expression of even a thousand degrees below zero has no meaning; no such condition exists in nature. Two hundred seventy-three degrees centigrade below freezing is the so-called absolute zero, the coldest temperature that may exist in all the universe. In experimenting with liquid hydrogen and helium, scientists succeeded in creating extremely low temperatures that were within a few degrees from absolute zero. Therefore, in this case, again man can most closely approach the extreme lowest, but the highest is immensely and incomparably superior to anything that ever could be approached by human beings.

These few basic facts about the material universe of God encourage the acceptance of a higher general outlook that confidently rejects the idea of deliberately inflicted everlasting agony. The analogy of the spiritual world with divine laws that control the material universe only suggests certain ideas. It is the Christian consciousness inspired not by the letter, but by the spirit of the

Gospel message that could not accept the idea that Christ, having suffered on Calvary, would deliberately inflict incomparably greater agony on a multitude of living beings. I faithfully believe that the suffering of Christ must be considered as being about the greatest possible in the universe. And in this case the mysterious meaning of this action may extend far beyond the destinies of earthly mankind.

Just as the darkness and cold that could be reached on the earth are practically the greatest possible, while light and power are but a negligible and insignificant fraction of what there is in the material heaven-universe of God, the same must be true with respect to the universe of higher eternal life. The evil, suffering and agony which we see on the earth are probably close to the greatest that may exist in the universe. But the happiness and blessing in the life of the higher order in the divine heaven-universe may and must be incomparably and infinitely higher, better and greater than any satisfaction or happiness that may be reached on the earth.

In general, it appears logical to summarize our ideas about the purpose of our earthly life as an immense gift, an opportunity given to a human being to develop a character and an individual personality which is willing, worthy and capable of survival in the higher order of existence. What this order means and what is the character of transition remains indeed a deep mystery beyond our faculties of understanding. The most we know about it are certain general and vague ideas that are left to us by religious leaders and are supported during some happy moments of our earthly existence by an inspired, intuitive inner feeling.

Nearly all religions compare God with the Sun and the action of His spiritual power with light. In this life the sunlight is, in general, the most important factor and causes nearly all natural processes on the surface of the earth. While normal men and most other creatures draw health and joy from sunlight, there are many forms of disease germs that are destroyed by this same sunlight if exposed to it directly.

I believe this to be an analogy with what the future holds for our little corner of the universe. Our earth is gradually moving along the road of time towards some definite event of immense importance. At present we are living in some lukewarm state of compromise, a mixture of good and evil, of truth and of lies. We are not yet exposed to the all-penetrating, all-powerful rays of spiritual light coming from the Most High Source. Some dense screen is apparently covering the earth through which only a very minor fraction of this light enters our almost complete darkness. Human beings in various ways have received some preliminary information about this light, but they were largely shielded by this screen from its direct action. This condition leaves human beings to develop their inner personalities as freely as they wish along the lines of eternal goodness and truth or in the opposite direction. The same conditions, namely, the temporary absence of direct divine light, most probably permit the development of some spiritual beings of negative characteristics. *All* earthly living beings must remain tem-

porarily under the screen for reasons that are perceived
only dimly by us, but which apparently are essential to
human freedom of will.

A large part of mankind takes this existence as
being more or less normal, appears to be satisfied by the
doubtful and extremely insecure achievements of human
progress, but still subconsciously has aspirations for some
different and better order to come. Others, spiritually and
intellectually inferior, call humanity to forget entirely
about any higher life and concentrate efforts and hopes on
the rearrangement of material things of this earthly existence only. The grave danger which this involves for the
neglected future life is unfortunately seldom realized in
its full meaning. But even in this life the tendencies that
were mentioned have never contributed to anything except a greatly increased disorder, injustice and suffering.

The best part of humanity at all times under
one form or another invariably regarded this existence as a
temporary exile. They felt and resented the screen that
separated them from the eternal source of life and spiritual
light. They wanted and prayed for the great event, the
fundamental change of conditions that would open the
spiritual light, which in turn would chase away and de-
stroy all spiritual darkness. The teaching of the Founder
of Christianity disclosed and explained this event and its
meaning and purpose as it has never been done before.
It disclosed that a profound mystery is connected with
human life in this world and particularly with the destinies
of men after this greatest event that will terminate the
present stage of the historical process. It also disclosed that
humanity is immensely indebted to Christ Himself in con-

nection with this event and the possibility of individual existence beyond it.

There is no doubt that the entire first part of the Lord's Prayer deals mainly with this final event that will mark the termination of the present era of compromise, suffering and of death and will open the new one of light, complete harmony, good will, happiness, and everlasting life. The strangest and most encouraging aspect of the prayer is that it assumes the person that pronounces it as already being under way into this happy, eternal existence. Of course, by our crime or foolishness, we may spoil our immense inheritance as we can ruin an earthly one, but the prayer indicates plainly that the infinite opportunity is offered; it is ours already, together with the incredible right to address the Creator, King and Owner of the Universe not by any of these true titles but by the simple words, "Our Father."

The ideas expressed assume a considerably wider meaning and can be much better understood now in the light of our present knowledge of the universe. It has been mentioned already that if we take the opening words as well as the second and third sentence of the first prayer in their direct logical meaning, the conclusion would be that the earth is not yet a part of the Kingdom of God, that the earth is still deprived of His presence and that the Will of God is not yet active on this earth to the extent or form in which it is exercised in the already existing Kingdom of God in Heaven. These conclusions hardly can be questioned unless we change the logical meaning of these sentences of the prayer. It is much easier to understand this if the meaning of the sentences is analyzed on the basis of modern information about the heaven-universe and the relative importance of our earth.

Taking the entire territory of the United States to represent the whole universe, our earth would be as a small glass test tube with, say, one cubic inch of volume. In true proportion, the earth would still be very much smaller, but for the present discussion, such relative scale may be taken to illustrate the case. Some Great Scientist placed inside the test tube the proper materials, created necessary conditions, sealed the test tube and left it in a laboratory until the expected reaction would take place. In line with such a picture, it is obvious that the Scientist is not inside the test tube but from the outside He sees and knows what is happening inside. In many chemical, as well as biological processes, the ordinary procedure would be to create conditions, place materials and leave them all alone for a while until the desired reaction is completed. Taking this as an analogy, we may assume further that the Great Scientist may temporarily curtail exercising His Will upon separate events inside the test tube. His Will in a general way has already been imposed, in view of His having arranged the whole experiment. He leaves the reaction to proceed in accordance with His laws until all valuable elements crystallize and become separated from worthless and poisonous by-products of the process. When this happens, the Great Scientist will break the sealed tube, place the valuable crystals where He wants them and order the worthless remnants destroyed.

The above story seeks to present a fair picture of the relative importance of the earth and of the heaven-universe from the standpoint of size and time. This is not difficult to understand but it is almost impossible to imagine that the difference is probably similar with respect to the now invisible spiritual and intellectual values connected with higher orders of living existence that inhabit this heaven-universe.

Man feels lifted to eminent heights of hope and gratitude to his Creator and Teacher who in some mysterious way opened the door from our little earth, that will eventually be destroyed with its contents, into the immensity and splendor of the heaven-universe. This is the deeply important and significant meaning of the first part of the Lord's Prayer.

On the preceding pages, the writer expressed his belief that the first part of the Lord's Prayer is devoted mainly to the final outcome of the earthly process and the eternal destiny of mankind in the Kingdom of God. In the way of a pronounced contrast with this aspect, the second part of the Prayer deals essentially with the needs and difficulties of the present time and of the immediate future only. Our bread is asked for "this day"; not even for tomorrow. The same is true with respect to the remaining two petitions.

Each of the three sentences deals with entirely different aspects of our earthly existence and, with reasonably wide understanding, they cover all material and spiritual needs of our present life.

THIS SENTENCE has first of all a direct meaning. It may be understood also as taking into consideration all other reasonable necessities such as a home, clothing, medical assistance, and so forth, that are just as necessary for our earthly existence as food. There is hardly any doubt that this sentence approves and even instructs man to work for the material necessities of himself and his family. A man can pray for assistance in any reasonable need of his life, but the prayer has no chance of being effective if the man himself does not contribute first all he can in work and effort to complete the part that he can do himself. A man who prepared his field and planted it can well pray for results and no one can prove that these prayers have no influence. But a prayer of an idle person that his field miraculously be planted for him would be quite hopeless. If, however, the person is ill or for any reason actually unable to do it himself, such prayer may well bring results in some indirect way.

It appears logical to consider that the sentence about "our daily bread" considers also our intellectual and spiritual needs. In a different way these factors are just as important for the life and proper development of human personality. The Founder of Christianity often referred to human desires and needs in the spiritual field as hunger or thirst and to His gifts as "bread" or "water." Therefore, as in the case of material necessities, prayer is fully legitimate, but must be preceded by an earnest effort on the part of man himself to do all he can in the way of intellectual and spiritual achievements; but he is entitled to ask —and must ask—for help and guidance in problems and situations which exceed his own competence and ability.

"... AND FORGIVE US OUR DEBTS AS WE FORGIVE OUR DEBTORS"

THIS SENTENCE has, primarily, a direct and obvious meaning, but in addition this same forgiveness and an attitude towards it has a bearing on the future life and our preparation for that life.

A sharp warning with a direct and positive meaning is included in the last five words of this sentence. It is a plain request to man to forgive his personal enemies, to cancel all ill thoughts against them before starting to pray for his own forgiveness. The request imposed by the Founder of Christianity in this sentence is definite, and the person who uses the prayer cannot disregard it without rendering his own prayer ineffective. The meaning of this request must not be extended beyond the well-indicated limits. A Christian monk of old times commenting on this subject said that a man must live in peace with all other men, even with his enemies, but not with the enemies of God. It appears certain that this, as well as other sentences of the Gospel, do not liberate man from his duty to denounce and resist such forces as are threatening some of the higher values. To determine what they are or to recognize the true enemies of God presents a different problem, the discussion of which is outside the present study. It is sufficient to mention in this connection that one who honestly seeks truth in these questions usually will be able to recognize it.

With further reference to this sentence, attention may be called again to the remarkable precision in the use of expressions that are characteristic of the Lord's Prayer. For instance, the wording, "Forgive us our sins as we forgive the sins of other men," would easily open the way to numbers of conflicting interpretations. But the actual sentence, "as we forgive our debtors," is definite and leaves no doubt as to its true meaning. We are ordered to forgive the harm done to ourselves. We are not authorized to forgive the insults or harm done to any other person.

It is interesting to note that the word *love*, which appears to be so prominently associated with Christian teachings, is not mentioned a single time in the Lord's Prayer. The teaching that we should love our enemies is one of the most frequently mentioned sentences of the Gospel. It is, however, not often remarked that this requirement is very seldom, if ever, fulfilled by men; and it was apparently not followed even by Christ Himself if we refer to the word *love* in its modern sense. While numerous instances in His life illustrate His unlimited sympathy and forgiveness, including even a prayer for the soldiers on Calvary, yet we have no grounds to say, for instance, that Christ loved the High Priests who were His real enemies. The discord that has been mentioned here is, however, not a real one. I personally believe it to be caused by the fact that the word *love*, which most certainly was correctly mentioned in the Gospels, had then a somewhat different meaning from the modern one. At present, love means mostly a sentiment and as such cannot be really subject to will power. The ancient meaning that existed at the time when the Gospels were written was more of the character of good will exercised toward some person. This can be done by an inner act of will power, and, therefore, could be requested by Christ from His followers and of course was always invariably maintained by Christ Himself.

The principal object of the phrase under discussion is the ultimate benefit to the person who pronounces the prayer, but it also includes immediate practical results in determining his attitude toward his fellows and in forcing him to cancel at least some of his bad sentiments and personal hatreds. This contributes to what we will call purifying the spiritual atmosphere; a process that is more important than most men usually realize.

"AND LEAD US NOT INTO TEMPTATION; BUT DELIVER US FROM EVIL"

THE UNLIMITED sympathy and good will of the Author of the Prayer toward mankind is widely known and accepted, but I believe that it is not sufficiently emphasized that He knew and understood humanity thoroughly and had not the slightest illusion concerning the limitations and sinfulness of mankind. The helplessness of man in the face of temptation, and the specific weaknesses that render each human being especially subject to some temptation, according to the particular weak links in his character, are taken for granted by the Author of the Prayer. He does not suggest a prayer for courage and power to resist temptation. Man is instructed to pray that the dangerous conditions be avoided.

In other words, strange as it sounds to many modern people, the Prayer instructs us to ask not for courage and determination to win a certain battle, but for the help of God to avoid that battle. Of the three propositions of the second prayer, this one contains the deepest mystery and, to my belief, touches the most important as well as the most dramatic factors of earthly existence. The origin and source of the greatest tragedies in the life of individuals as well as of nations can be traced to the mysterious factors discussed in this eleven-word sentence more than to any other cause. This statement is in contradiction with the now widely accepted materialistic interpretation of life and history, but I believe it to be much closer to the truth.

The extreme difficulty of complete understanding of this part of the prayer will in no way limit the value of our using it as long as we have confidence in its Author. The situation may be stated simply as follows: we are warned of a danger, we are informed that our personal forces are inadequate to resist the enemy and we are instructed to call for the help of God. It is obvious that man must nevertheless do all he can to resist any evil temptations, but he must not expect to be successful in really important cases unless he asks and receives divine assistance.

The principal subject contained in the first half of the sentence is expressed by the word "temptation." The meaning of this word is generally clear. There are various legitimate explanations, but it may be summed up as a sort of proposed deal in which values of lower order are purchased at the sacrifice of values of higher order. The main subject of the second half of the sentence is connected with the word *evil*. The whole sentence obviously mentions two phases of one single subject and indicates that the ideas of temptation and of evil are interconnected. It is the meaning of the word *evil* that represents a highly controversial subject and one full of mystery.

A very interesting discussion of this subject is included in the last work of V. Solovieff, who was a prominent student of religious philosophy in Russia at the end of the nineteenth century. The *Three Conversations* were written by him in 1900, only a few months before his death. Attributing profound importance to this subject, Solovieff begins the introduction of his story in the following way.

"Is evil only a weakness, a natural deficiency that will gradually disappear by itself as long as goodness increases, or is it a real, active power that controls the world by the use of temptations so that to resist it successfully, one must have a point of support in another order of existence?"

Solovieff outlined well the·two·different views which exist on this important subject. This distinction is not often realized and many modern, even religious, people take the first of the two propositions for granted and consider the last one as a long-outlived prejudice. In this case, namely, if evil is considered as a weakness, as a lack in goodness and intelligence, or as an inheritance· of our animal ancestry, all of which are part of our own nature, then indeed an increase in intelligence and good will in men themselves would be a reliable and sufficient remedy. The help of God would remain useful but not positively necessary.

The subject under discussion is more in the spiritual than in the material or intellectual realm. This makes a direct study by our intellectual faculties and direct logical proofs impossible, but while the solution of it remains a question of faith, a better understanding of the true meaning of the controversy may be obtained by the use of the well-known method of analogies with events which take place on a lower plane of existence. Let us consider the physical part of man—his body—and let us assume that factors contributing to health and power are representing goodness and good will, while factors causing suffering and illness are representative of evil. It appears that this assumption of the similarity between spiritual and physical areas of life is reasonable. Could we consider that every illness can be resisted by simply improving the general health and by providing better food, housing, fresh air, rest, and so forth? It is well-known that this is not the case. We know that suffering and sickness caused by undernourishment, overwork, lack of fresh air, injuries, and similar causes, can be successfully treated by such methods. This is saying that simple goodness and good will alone are sufficient to drive out the "evil" in these cases.

We are also familiar with sickness of a totally different nature. Let us consider cholera or some forms of pestilence. When epidemics of diseases happen, it is the young and strong whom they strike and who die just the same as the weak or crippled. The best food, clothing, rest, and so forth, in other words factors that our analogy considers as representing human goodness and good will, are practically of no value to resist such diseases or prevent their propagation.

Certain diseases of this group are incomparably more terrible than any and all of the first group mentioned. Cases have been known in history when more than half of the population of a country was destroyed by an epidemic; when the entire population of villages was killed by a disease and wolves and other beasts came to feed on the bodies because there was no one left to bury them. Even a comparatively less dangerous disease of this group—smallpox—only a hundred years ago in civilized countries was causing every year more deaths than the greatest number of men killed during a year in the First World War.

All attempts to combat these diseases were practically worthless until it was discovered that the illness represented, not a weakness or deficiency of the human body, but the attack of an evil force—in this case, the disease germs which penetrate from outside and cause suffering and death by the poison which they develop. At present in all civilized countries medical science has such infectious diseases well under control, and we can hardly imagine the disasters caused by this physical evil in the past.

To what extent the above picture taken from the material plane is similar to the one in the spiritual, we cannot know because we do not know sufficiently this second plane. Assuming that there is some analogy between the physical and the spiritual evil, we still could not expect the one to be a scale model of the other. The following few conclusions, however, appear reasonable.

The presence of evil in the physical and spiritual levels of human existence on this earth is obvious. Several of our wisest men have expressed surprise that there should be so much of it. We saw that in the physical plane evil comes from two completely different sources, one connected with weakness and deficiency of our own body, the other being the result of penetration and poisoning by a totally alien, evil force. There are no good reasons for denying the possibility of the case being to some extent similar with respect to the spiritual order of our earthly life.

With reference to resistance, we saw that in the physical area the decisive victory was won when intellects like Pasteur's took command in the fight against the terrible physical enemy. Such intellect is a power of higher order contrasted with that of bacteria. Considering that contrast and pursuing our analogy further we may assume the existence of mysterious evil forces in the spiritual order of life on our earth. According to the ideas of Solovieff, man can successfully resist these forces only if he has a point of support in a spiritual order higher than his own.

The above-mentioned conclusion of Solovieff must be understood as referring to the cases when men or nations are confronted with the really serious manifestations of evil. Such trivial trespasses as gambling, drinking, vice and crime, can and must be resisted by an act of will power of man himself and it is easy to point to a number of persons with no religious beliefs who never ask for the help of God but, nevertheless, are able to maintain a respectable life and, as far as all outward appearances go, to resist such temptations.

The question what is evil is frequently answered by references to gambling, drinking, vice and crime. Such a reply cannot be disputed, but it points only to the secondary manifestations of evil. Almost every one will take for granted that drunkards, gamblers and criminals are worthless for God and harmful for men, but few people recognize that figuratively they are also of little value for the devil because the really dangerous aggressions of evil come mainly from another direction.

In what was one of the greatest encounters between goodness and evil, namely, in the events that resulted in Calvary, the criminals, drunkards, and gamblers, as far as we know, took no part. The fierce hatred of Christ which was responsible for the tragedy was nursed mainly by church-going bible-reading puritans and by fanatical revolutionaries. Both groups acted for reasons which they largely believed to be worthy, and correctly recognized in Christ their greatest adversary. It would be a mistake to explain the actions of the enemies of Christ simply by their selfishness and offended self-esteem. The moving power behind the great tragedy was a form of idealism and patriotism which became captured and misled by a truly sinister, evil, ideological influence.

Many of the Jews of that time dreamed about a Messiah King who would not only liberate their nation but would conquer and dominate the world. The existence of such aspirations is confirmed by the following interesting historical document:

"What did most elevate them in undertaking this war [the rebellion against Rome] was an ambiguous oracle that was also found in their sacred writings, how about that time one from their country should become governor of the habitable earth."[1]

The same idea forms the subject of the last and main temptation of Christ in the wilderness:

"And the devil . . . shewed unto Him all the kingdoms of the world in a moment of time. And the devil said unto Him, all this power will I give thee, and the glory of them" (Luke 4:5-6).

Christ rejected and condemned the ambitious proposition. He recognized in it not a Divinely ordained destiny but an evil temptation. Christ inflicted great harm to the wished-for rebellion by giving a completely differ-

[1]Josephus Flavius, Book IV, page 253, Edition 1820.

ent interpretation of the Messianic ideal, thereby causing perplexity and division among the people in face of the approaching uprising.

The writer is convinced that the uncompromising stand of Christ in this ideological conflict was the main cause of the popular fury against Him which resulted in the shouting, "Let Him be crucified. . . . His blood be on us and on our children" (Matthew 27:23, 25). The same profoundly unfortunate and popular ideology was responsible for the ill-fated uprising of 67–71 A.D. that resulted in the destruction of Jerusalem and an unprecedented national disaster.

This case was not an exception. Several of the greatest assaults of evil during the whole history of mankind can best be explained by causes of similar nature. The true Mammon for the triumph of which even unselfish and apparently good men are willing to disregard the fundamental commandments of Christ and are ready to lie, hate and kill, can be much better identified with the lust for political domination than with desires for personal wealth or pleasure. The most shameless deceits and most formidable mass murders can be traced to evil ideological causes much more than to any individual sin or crime.

There is no doubt that all the pirates, bandits and criminals of the whole world have spilled during a thousand years less tears and blood and caused less moral degradation than the Communists in Russia did within a quarter of a century. And yet, according to a correct remark of D. Merejkovsky,[2] some of the Bolsheviks are honest

[2]*The Kingdom of the Anti-Christ,* by D. Merejkovsky, page 18. Russian edition published by Drei Maskeu Verlag in 1921.

and sincere and these, he adds, are the most dreadful ones.

The two cases that were mentioned are among the greatest historical manifestations of evil on a large scale. There is also a multitude of different individual cases when separate human beings may be confronted with evil temptations of various kinds, some time only of an inner nature which, nevertheless, may be serious enough to justify and necessitate calling for Divine assistance. In general the subject of evil is profoundly important and must be recognized as a real danger in the life of individuals as well as nations.

We will now attempt to determine directly what is evil and what are the most important and dangerous manifestations of it in the earthly process. In the Gospel we find the following powerful and sharp sentence:

"He [the devil] was a murderer from the beginning, and abode not in the truth, because there is no truth in him. When he speaketh a lie, he speaketh of his own: for he is a liar, and the father of it" (John 8:44).

Dostoyevsky, through his Grand Inquisitor, calls him, "the wise and dreadful spirit of self-destruction and non-existence."[3]

A talented, modern Russian author, Ivan Lukash, impressed by the terrible realities of godless Communism, writes:

"The devil is a murderer, an extinguisher of the spirit and of thought, a snake that is stinging life. . . . Oh, I understand, I see the devil in my Russia, and in the whole world . . . the devil is the dead matter, the dust of the earth that is suffocating the spirit, that is distorting by

[3] *The Brothers Karamazov,* Modern Library, Random House, page 261.

his lies . . . in the name of corrupting flesh, the eternal Word and eternal Thought . . . the devil is the inspiration that was crushed under the dead immensity of the material earth."

This profound, inspired analysis is followed by a severe reproach addressed to the men who serve the unworthy objective.

"I understand that matter is always struggling with thought, that the masses of burned out slag are stifling the universal fire, but I do not understand all this rabble, all the servants of the earthly matter whoever they are, professors, false prophets, revolutionists who, like blind mice, want to replace the principle of eternal life in the spirit by the principle of eternal death in the matter."[4]

In line with the above-mentioned statements the main manifestation of evil consists in falsehood and murder, while the fundamental consequence of it may be understood as the poisoning, crippling and destruction of the spiritual component of the human being, which in turn would make everlasting life impossible. While the ravaging results remain unexpected and unknown because the consequences could be learned only on the other side of physical death, yet great disasters may happen even in this life when the moral and spiritual atmosphere becomes excessively befogged by godlessness, and when men deprive themselves of divine guidance and protection from evil. Such is the true inner meaning of the disastrous events that happened in Russia during the last quarter of a century.

According to our beliefs we may accept or deny any reality to the first cause of evil. We may con-

[4]*The House of the Dead,* published by Miedni Vsadnik, pages 141,142.

sider that it does not exist outside the consciousness of man. But whether the first cause is true or imaginary the consequences and manifestations of evil are tragically real in this world.

Modern humanity in general does not realize the value of the protection given by Christ against the mysterious spiritual dangers even in this life. Mankind can in this respect be compared to a child that was bitten by a mad dog and does not comprehend the gravity of the danger and the value of the life-saving inoculation that is given it by a wise and benevolent Doctor.

The writer believes that the last petition of the Lord's Prayer refers mainly to a mysterious and dangerous evil influence that is capable of assuming a large variety of aspects and may even appear under the guise of service to idealistic or humanitarian principles. The whole historical process and the tragic experience of our time indicate that human intellect and highest scientific education are unable to recognize and powerless to resist the sinister danger of spiritual evil, while scientific discoveries and engineering inventions are liable to become the servants of evil, helping to spread lies, fear, hatred and murder on an unprecedented scale. A multitude of facts of such nature appear to confirm the idea of Solovieff that men and nations are unable to resist for any appreciable length of time the deadly poison of spiritual evil unless they have a point of support in a higher order of existence. The writer believes that such support, in other words divine guidance and protection, is asked in the sentence, "And lead us not into temptation, but deliver us from evil."

"FOR THINE IS THE KINGDOM AND THE POWER AND THE GLORY FOR EVER"

In the three Gospels, near the beginning, there is an account of a strange and mysterious event known as the temptation of Christ. There were no witnesses in the wilderness, therefore the account must be the story as told by Christ Himself to His Disciples, a fact which emphasizes the great importance of this event. It is most probable that major decisions taken by the Founder of Christianity at that time determined not only the course of His own earthly life but also the general course of the history of mankind from that period on. The meaning of this strange dialogue in the desert has been discussed by the great Russian writer-philosopher, Dostoyevsky, in his profoundly interesting Legend of the Grand Inquisitor[1] according to which the story of temptation as given in the Gospels represents a very short summary of two conflicting points of view covering all major controversies which determine the tragedies and destinies of mankind in this life; discords that are deeply rooted in human nature but

[1] *The Brothers Karamazov*, Modern Library, Random House, pages 255–272.

also extend or at least are projected into the higher order of existence.

There is a pronounced analogy between the second part of the prayer and the ideas and even expressions of the story of temptation. This can be seen from the following table of texts.

THE SECOND PART OF THE LORD'S PRAYER		THE STORY OF TEMPTATION
"give us this day our daily *BREAD*	*BREAD* ·	. . . command that these stones be made *BREAD* (Matthew 4:3).
"and *LEAD* us not into *TEMPTATION,* but deliver us from *EVIL*	*LEAD—LED TEMPTATION —TEMPTED EVIL—DEVIL*	Then was Jesus *LED* up of the spirit into the wilderness to be *TEMPTED* of the *DEVIL* (Matthew 4:1).
"For thine is the *KINGDOM*	*KINGDOM— KINGDOMS*	And the devil, taking him up into an high mountain, shewed unto him all the *KING-DOMS* of the world in a moment of time (Luke 4:5).
"and the *POWER* and the *GLORY* for ever.	*POWER GLORY*	And the devil said unto him, All this *POWER* will I give thee, and the *GLORY* of them (Luke 4:6).

There seems to be little doubt that the same fundamental factors which influence the acts and deter-

mine the destinies of individuals and of nations are referred
to in both documents. The story of the temptation gives
a very brief account of the strange conference at which
future destinies of mankind were discussed but no agreement was reached. The second part of the Lord's Prayer
refers to the same factors, but this time from the standpoint
of the everyday life of an individual.

In the final question of the temptation, the
adversary of Christ claimed to possess and control the
Kingdoms and the power and the glory of this world. The
Founder of Christianity did not dispute that claim but instructed us to make a reply in the conclusion of the prayer
every time we pronounce it, "For thine is the kingdom,
and the power, and the glory. . . ."

An analysis of these extremely important questions discloses a point which does not permit a convincing
explanation as long as the earth is considered the major and
most important part of the universe. The first part of the
prayer discloses that the Kingdom of God does not yet
exist on the earth. The story of the temptation mentions
the claim of the devil to own and control this world. The
claim seems to be justified unfortunately by too many
events of ancient as well as modern times; it is even ad-
mitted in many passages of the Gospel. But, the conclud-
ing verse of the great prayer says "for thine *is* the kingdom, and the power, and the glory." The sentence says *is*,
not even "will be." Yet the standing of a kingdom can indeed be questioned if on a major part of its territory the
will of the King is largely disregarded and if an alien, hostile power is permitted to exercise its control. The picture

is not clear and does not become any clearer with the ideas of sin being introduced.

All these contradictions disappear at once and the meaning of the great prayer becomes clear and comprehensible as soon as we consider the true universe of God in the light of modern science. The zone occupied by the hostile power, namely our earth, shrinks immediately to utter insignificance and the evil power that claims to control it is no longer another sovereign of comparable standing that disputes the power.

Figuratively speaking, it is probably merely a nest of rats that remain below the floor of a little country cabin, located somewhere in the woods and for some reason temporarily isolated by a sort of quarantine from the rest of the vast kingdom. The great King Himself is well informed in His immense, wonderful palace about all that happens and also about this little detail. He leaves it alone for a while knowing that when the proper time comes He will order the floor of the little cabin removed and the pests destroyed. In line with such understanding the future holds for every one either isolation and eventual destruction, together with the pernicious spiritual refuse of the earthly process, or free everlasting life in the light and splendor of the heaven-universe.

This outline of ideas inspired by the Greatest of Prayers may now be concluded with the following brief review.

The words of address are a bold claim of being children of God. In contrast with them, the next sentence "hallowed be Thy name," reflects modesty, indicating the infinite and eternal difference between man and the King of the universe Whom the former has just addressed by the words, "Our Father."

The two following sentences namely: "Thy kingdom come." "Thy will be done in earth as it is in heaven"—are again raising man to immense heights of potential importance. They include a strange aspect. Assuming that similar words would be addressed by a humble subject to a medieval autocrat, it would be well to expect an indignant reply that his kingdom would exist and his will would be exercised irrespective of whether some impertinent slave wants it or not. And yet incredible as it sounds, the free consent of man has apparently a meaning in the question of the future coming of the Kingdom of God. The importance and dignity which are assumed by man when he addresses this direct petition to the King of the universe about the final outcome of the whole earthly process are seldom recognized.

When man pronounces these bold and significant words, he rises above all the needs, ambitions, humiliations, outrages, all the apparent triumphs of wickedness. Man confidently recognizes the solution of all contradictions of this world, the true justification of the turbulent process of earthly life, and the only really worthy objective of it. Man concentrates his attention and aspiration and reunites them with the will of God in respect to the final, eternal objective of the whole process of creation of mankind. In praying about the future divine kingdom of eternal life, truth and glory, man indirectly expresses his own hope of entering it; otherwise, it would be a cruel disappointment to pray about the triumph of divine right-eousness if the man himself were to be condemned never to see it and if all his individual conscious existence would be limited to the present earthly order of darkness and suffering.

The second part of the Lord's Prayer, as has been pointed out, is completely different and covers the immediate needs and dangers of this life. The sentence about "our daily bread" can well be understood as refer-ring to all material, intellectual and spiritual needs of our earthly existence. The petitions about "forgiveness" and about "temptation," while referring to inner spiritual events and dangers of the immediate future, are essential mainly with respect to the influence which these inner acts of will power and passion may have on the eternal life of the individual.

The prayer begins and is concluded by simple and reverent expressions of praise to Divine Providence. As if reflecting the whole process of creation, the first sentence refers only to God, "hallowed be Thy name," while the conclusion mentions the "kingdom, power and glory." This may well be understood to refer to the Divine wisdom and power which have created and control the whole material and spiritual universe.

The Lord's Prayer was composed by its Au-thor for our earthly life with the purpose of guiding us across the turbulent and dramatic process of our spiritual birth. When that period is over on our earth and possibly also on other similar planets, the object of the complete prayer will be fulfilled. But it is not impossible that in ren-dering praise and glory to their Creator the happy beings of the higher order of existence will still be using the following three sentences of the Lord's Prayer that are and will remain beyond any limitations of space or time.

> *Our Father which art in heaven,*
> *Hallowed be thy name. . . .*
> *For thine is the kingdom, and the power,*
>   *and the glory, for ever.*

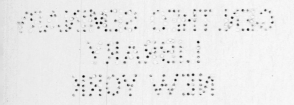